Kingdom First

Bible Studies
For the Kingdom-
New Covenant Church

Volume I

Stan Newton

Kingdom First
Bible Studies for the Kingdom-
New Covenant Church
By Dr. Stan Newton

© 2018 by Stan Newton

Endorsement from Solid Rock Church

Sedona, Arizona

Stan Newton's *Kingdom First* Bible course is a three-part scriptural exegesis with historical-contextual accuracy based on the "Dream of God!" The course takes you through to the fulfillment of His dream completing the circle of transformation with the student. The study covers the dream of God beginning in Genesis and takes people through to the revelation of the whole picture contained in the vision of the Father for mankind.

Solid Rock chose this study because we want our congregation to grow in greater understanding and knowledge of the better new covenant, kingdom, and eschatology. We have utilized this study in our church, using the discussion questions at the end of each chapter as a tool to apply the gospel of the Kingdom principles in the everyday life of a believer.

Patricia Garitson,
Kingdom Revivalist
Shapeyourdestinyimage.com
www.solidrockchurchofsedona.com

Table of Contents

Preface

Advancing the Reign of Christ through biblical education is the goal of *Kingdom First*. Audacious as it seems, I am convinced the 'renewing of the mind' through biblical understanding is key to bringing the church closer to its calling and mission from God. These lessons set the kingdom of God within time - our time and history. The kingdom is within and among us; it is our message and our guarantee that God is a covenant keeping God.

Within churches which embrace charismatic gifts there are tendencies to elevate experience over the study of Scripture. What is needed now is not the devaluing of our spiritual experiences but the raising of our level of understanding the word of God. Understanding how the kingdom of God works in Scripture will sharpen our calling, empower our mission, refocus the church, enhance discipleship and deepen our worship. It is time to see the kingdom of God placed where it belongs - as the central cord that unites the Bible. It is time to "Seek first the kingdom of God."

Kingdom First is a series of teachings in three volumes. The first begins with Genesis and takes us through the key Old Testament Scriptures about the kingdom. In Volume II we start with John the Baptist and study the birth, life, miracles and teachings of Jesus. We focus on His kingship and how He viewed the kingdom of God in His ministry. The final volume begins with the pouring out of the Holy Spirit and looks at the early church and how we are the heirs of those who advanced the kingdom of God in the earth.

For Teachers: *Kingdom First* is a teaching manual which does not go into detail on each subject. Therefore, if you are a teacher, I would advise that you read my two books, *Glorious Kingdom* and *Glorious Covenant*. Also, reading Jonathan Welton's *Understanding the Whole Bible* would be helpful. If students are not familiar with basic terms in eschatology or in the study of the covenants, a summary of terms may be needed before beginning. God is restoring key areas of Scripture in our generation to prepare the church to advance the kingdom of God. My prayer is that these lessons will help in that effort.

Stan Newton
Sofia, Bulgaria

Lesson 1
The Dream of God

We all have dreams. Personal dreams. Dreams of world peace. Dreams of a perfect family, career or church. Have we forgotten though, that God also has a dream? His dream is recorded in the Bible's first chapter; Genesis 1. Our beginning must align with how God begins His written story.

Too many trace the story of redemption back to Genesis chapter 3, but that point of beginning, throughout the generations, has caused a distortion of how we perceive the key elements of what we traditionally call 'The Gospel.'

When we begin with the 'fall' and then build everything around 'sin' we neglect where God's plan truly begins. God's dream and our story begin in Genesis 1.

> *In the beginning, God created the heavens and the earth. The earth was without form and void, and darkness was over the face of the deep. And the Spirit of God was hovering over the face of the waters.*
>
> *And God said, "Let there be light," and there was light.* (Genesis 1:1-3)
>
> *Then God said, "Let us make man in our image, after our likeness. And let them have dominion over the fish of the sea and over the birds of the heavens and over the livestock and over all the earth and over every creeping thing that creeps on the earth.*
>
> *So God created man in his own image, in the image of God he created him; male and female he created them. And God blessed them. And God said to them,*

"Be fruitful and multiply and fill the earth and subdue it, and have dominion over the fish of the sea and over the birds of the heavens and over every living thing that moves on the earth." (Genesis 1:26-28)

After different aspects of creation, the Scripture says, *"And God saw that it was good."* (Gen.1:10, 12, 18, 21, 25, 31)

Here is what we learn in the first chapter of our Bible:

1. God is the Creator of all things

Since all of creation has a Creator - the one and true God - this eliminates all worldviews built around evolutionary theories, humanism, atheism, and any belief system which denies the God of creation.

In addition, this God of creation is the God of Israel. There is one God, the God of Abraham, Isaac and Jacob. This is the consistent testimony of both the Old and the New Testaments.

The One,who creates is the One, who makes the rules. Since there is only one Creator, it reminds us there is only one true God.

2. The Creation of God is good

What God created is good. What He created is filled with beauty, wisdom, usefulness and purpose. God delights in what He creates and that incudes you. Redemptive history can be simply stated as 'God's plan through His Son, to win you back.'

Creation of Time

An aspect of creation is the creation of time. We can presuppose that before the creation God was in a timeless environment. The debate continues today if God lives 'in time' or 'outside of time.' I remember in about 4th or 5th grade our Sunday School teacher told us:

"When God looks down from heaven, he sees Moses crossing the Red Sea, Elijah preforming miracles, Daniel in the lion's den, Jesus suffering on the cross and God also sees us."

I was not old enough nor had sufficient knowledge to question my teacher, yet, it made little sense and it made me wonder, with so much to see, if God could really see me. I do not believe God looks down from heaven to see Moses crossing the Red Sea. If He wants to see Moses, most likely He is not far away. If God wants to see Jesus, well, Scriptures make it clear - there Jesus is, sitting at God's right hand. Jesus is not hanging on the cross for all eternity.

Time is a creation of God. Time is called *good.* Therefore, time is not our enemy. If we see 'time' as 'fallen' along with all of creation, then out task is to 'redeem time' in the fullest new creation sense. What this means our imagination can only speculate. I suspect that we have much to learn.

3. God created humanity to bear His 'image.'

In our modern culture the problem of identity looms large. People seek out various identities often in reaction to their peers. We, as God's people, are the direct creation of God. We carry His image. We carry His glory. Parts of our personalities can even be traced back to the traits of the triune God. The beginning of spiritual growth begins with knowing who we are. We are children of God, created to display His beauty, wisdom, love, power and grace to the created world. Even when we are not acting 'God-like' we still have His image stamped on us. Our primary calling in life is to be 'image bearers.'

4. We are created with similar (not exact) attributes

Some people attempt to take our stamp of God-likeness and make themselves God. We are God-like, but we are not God! We tend to create 'God in our image' and then live, making our own rules about life. All humanity is created as a

11

facsimile of our Creator. Yet we must not think we are equal to God or that we are carrying His exact attributes. We do not. Even before the fall, Adam and Eve did not possess everything which God possessed.

What do humans carry because of this 'God stamp?' First, we are creative. The first act we know of God is creation. All people have a touch of this creative side, but especially artists, writers, poets, musicians and all those who seem to draw from the unknown and unseen and bring it into our world. I would add theologians and those who dive deep in Scripture to bring out truths never seen before. Second, we have minds; we have basic intellect. Third, we are not just physical beings; we are 'spiritual beings.'

5. We are charged with a dominion mandate

We are God's highest order in His created world. Animals are not in charge. As much as we love animals and desire to protect them they are not given any dominion mandate. Humans are chosen to carry the responsibility for God's new world. The word *dominion* can cast imaginations of domination, if we are not careful. We are not called to destroy our rivers, oceans and forests, just because we have the power, but we are called to be faithful stewards over God's beautiful earth.

When we begin to comprehend our task in 'dominion' we then get our first clue to the fuller meaning of 'salvation.' Salvation is more than getting a ticket to heaven; it is being restored to God's dream of having a family to represent Him, in all His glorious aspects, to all creation. We have a common calling, a vocation as a people of God, to renew the world.

6. God desires our companionship

God likes us and desires to spend time with us. This is not a weakness in God, but something that reveals His heart towards us. In the garden, God was waiting every evening. Even when our first parents disobeyed and felt fear and unworthiness, there was God, wanting to talk with them. God did not separate Himself from Adam and Eve; it was Adam and Eve who did the separating. Salvation is many things and this concept of companionship with His people is foundational. If we see 'salvation' as only a legal judgment allowing us access into heaven, we are missing the point. In addition to salvation, we will see that 'covenant' is more than an agreement - it's also based upon a relationship.

7. God has a dream for His created people and His creation

If we learn anything from Genesis 1 it should be clear that God has a plan for planet earth and His 'image bearers.' The fall never changed this plan. It remains even today. Those Bible teachers who stress '*This world is not my home*' overlook the purpose of why God desired a 'physical universe' and a people with 'physical bodies.' There are no plans to destroy and start over, as some have presumed. The plan is to transform, renew and create the spiritual attributes of heaven on earth. God has a dream for this earth. We should also.

8. We see the beginning of Covenant

Although the early chapters of Genesis do not mention the word 'covenant,' we see the simple foundation of covenant. God instructed Adam and Eve about their life in the garden, with multitudes of opportunities and a single 'do not eat.' According to their choice God would then apply different parameters on how life would proceed. As the story continues in the Bible, we see 'covenant' take on a central role as He relates to His people and then finally, in Jesus, we have the new covenant, which radically changes everything.

9. New Testament application of God as Creator

With this point we are jumping a little ahead, but we need to mention how the New Testament apostles used 'God is the Creator' to enhance Jesus as a member of the triune God. The Jews were dogmatic that the God of Israel created the world. This gave them arguing authority over pagan nations. How did the New Testament writers address this? What they did, and very skillfully, was to wrap and center Jesus into the creation story. Several passages bear this out.

> *He is the image of the invisible God, the firstborn of all creation. For by him all things were created, in heaven and on earth, visible and invisible, whether thrones or dominions or rulers or authorities—all things were created through him and for him.* (Colossians 1:15-16)

> *In the beginning was the Word, and the Word was with God, and the Word was God. He was in the beginning with God. All things were made through him, and without him was not any thing made that was made.* (John 1:1-3)

10. The God of Israel is the Creator of the World

The biblical writers used this argument all through the Old Testament. Other gods were creations of men, they were made of wood, metals, and stone. They had no mind and no life. Therefore, they had no power over the human condition. To the contrary, Israel's God is the One, who created heaven and earth. Therefore, He is not only God over Israel, but over the whole world. Therefore, Israel was to be a 'light' to the nations.

God's goal was to renew the world through Israel. Yet, as the story unfolded, it was Israel which needed renewing. How would God get everything back on track? How would Israel be renewed or restored? There is only one answer; through the Messiah.

In summary of this first lesson and especially dealing with our attributes as God's 'image bearers' I will quote an article by Dick Staub.

> "When we fully grasp what it means to bear God's image, we are at once struck with the grandeur of our possibilities and the tragedy

14

of our unrealized potential. To be fully human is to fully reflect God's creative, spiritual, intelligent, communicative, relational, moral and purposeful capacities, and to do so holistically and synergistically. Furthermore, though all humans possess these God-like capacities, each of us has the potential to express them distinctively, because God's image has been imprinted uniquely on each of us. In God's infinite creativity there are no duplicates; *you* are the only *you* there ever were or ever will be." [1]

Discussion and Questions

1. Discuss what you think may have been God's purposes in creating a physical environment and then placing a new type of beings, humans, on planet earth. Why was heaven not enough?

2. What other attributes do we have as humans, that we share with God? How are we different?

3. How does the 'dominion' carry over into the New Covenant?

4. Why was it important for the New Testament authors to place Jesus into the story of Israel?

5. If it is God's dream to have a people on earth who bear His image and be His family, why is it so many Evangelicals center their hope around heaven?

6. Discuss how we can 'redeem time?' Does God live 'in time' or 'out of time'?

Footnotes
[1] Reprinted by permission of the publisher, John Wiley & Sons, Inc., from About You, by Dick Staub. This article was adapted from pages 29-37. Copyright © 2010 by John Wiley & Sons, Inc.

Lesson 2
Dream Interrupted

Now the serpent was more crafty than any other beast of the field that the Lord God had made. He said to the woman, "Did God actually say, 'You shall not eat of any tree in the garden'?" And the woman said to the serpent, "We may eat of the fruit of the trees in the garden, but God said, 'You shall not eat of the fruit of the tree that is in the midst of the garden, neither shall you touch it, lest you die.'"

But the serpent said to the woman, "You will not surely die. For God knows that when you eat of it your eyes will be opened, and you will be like God, knowing good and evil." So when the woman saw that the tree was good for food, and that it was a delight to the eyes, and that the tree was to be desired to make one wise, she took of its fruit and ate, and she also gave some to her husband who was with her, and he ate. Then the eyes of both were opened, and they knew that they were naked. And they sewed fig leaves together and made themselves loincloths.

And they heard the sound of the Lord God walking in the garden in the cool of the day, and the man and his wife hid themselves from the presence of the Lord God among the trees of the garden. But the Lord God called to the man and said to him, "Where are you?" And he said,

"I heard the sound of you in the garden, and I was afraid, because I was naked, and I hid myself." He said, "Who told you that you were naked? Have you eaten of the tree of which I commanded you not to eat?" The man said, "The woman whom you gave to be with me, she gave me fruit of the tree, and I ate." Then the Lord God said to the woman, "What is this that you have done?" The woman said, "The serpent deceived me, and I ate." (Genesis 3:1-13)

The 'image bearers' now take a wrong path. Getting back on God's path is the story of salvation. How God gets His people back on track is the unfolding of covenant.

The goal of covenant is the kingdom

Once we are on the God designed path, we are ready to begin the great adventure of walking and fellowshipping with God and collaborating with Him in this great quest; His kingdom on earth. Yet, before we can be back on track with God and His dream for us, the issue of sin must be dealt with.

What are the three kingdom traits we found in Genesis 1?

1. Relationship / Fellowship
2. Being God's Image Bearers
3. The Work of Dominion

When Adam fell, an obstacle was placed in front of humanity. It was sin. With all the attention 'sin' gets in the church, we might conclude its power and influence are unstoppable. We strive to stop sinning. Preachers tell us constantly to stop sinning. We look down on others who sin, and on it goes. Sin has taken over as a central theme in the church.

Because 'forgiveness of sin' was offered, and proclaimed in the New Testament we must approach this phrase not from our perspective, but from that of a first century Jew. When this is done and passages about sin are seen in their historical context, then, at least I hope, sin will find its place within the larger story of God. Once we accomplish this, sin can then be viewed not as the 'uncontrollable force' but as part of the package of what Jesus defeated on the cross.

What is Sin?
When we attach a modern definition to sin, it unfortunately leads us away from the core message of the Gospel. We see 'sin' as personal moral failure. The message in the Bible about 'sin' is more comprehensive; it defeats 'sin.' Now, this includes all our individual sins, but also it defeats the power of sin. What needed to be reversed was the sin nature of Adam. Now, Jesus the last Adam has done exactly that through His death on the cross.

To understand sin and how it interrupted the dream of God, we need a definition.

The Greek word for sin is 'hamartia.' The primary meaning is simply 'missing the mark.' When we sin, we miss the point of God's calling, our function as 'image-bearers.' It is less about 'moral failure' and more about being high-jacked to live a 'lesser life.' When we 'hit the mark' it means we are living as the royal kingdom priests we are called to be. When we 'hit the mark' the church shines as God's light to the nations. When we 'hit the mark' we show the faithfulness of God. Far too many in the church are so focused on individual moral failure - what we call sin - and abandon our 'kingdom vocational calling.'

Sin has consequences, serious ones. It takes us away from worship of the true Creator and leads us to erect idols of all sorts to follow. These idols become our captors and enslave us. How will we be delivered? Jesus died on a cross, so we can be set free and transferred into the kingdom of Jesus.

Sin distorts everything. The lens we use to discern, to evaluate life and even to understand God are marred and out of focus. Humanity moves through life in a fog-like existence. It is only in the 'New Creation' through Jesus, that we are set free. We are free to see God as He is. We are free to explore His profound purposes in everything we touch. We are free to dream again. Not the dreams of a distorted soul, but to dream God's Dream.

Discussion and Questions

1. Discuss, "Where does sin come from?" Did the serpent bring sin into the garden? Are Adam and Eve victims, or are they 'morally responsible' for their decision? Find some passages in the New Testament that clarify the question of where sin comes from.

2. How did the snake get Eve and then Adam to disobey the commands of God?

3. "When we sin, does God leave us?"

We have heard from many pulpits that God cannot look at sin, and therefore when we sin, He withdraws from us. Is this true? What happens to believers when they sin?

4. When God forgave our sins, is it only our *past* sins or our *present* and *future* sins as well? Does God forgive only sins before the moment of salvation, and afterwards it depends on individual repentance for each subsequent sin? What if we forget a sin or do not even recognize a thought or action as being sinful?

You can refer to the following Scriptures to assist in the discussion.

- Romans 5:18-19
- Romans 7:7-8
- Galatians 5:1 What is the connection between slavery and sin?

- I John 1:5-9 Is there a difference between 'being forgiven' for our sins and 'being cleansed from all unrighteousness'?

5. When we proclaim the Gospel, how should the aspect of 'sin' be presented?

6. Discuss why God took several covenants (not just one) to get us back on the kingdom path.

Lesson 3
A Chosen People

We now arrive at the part of the story where a key individual of the Bible is introduced. His name is Abraham. Many men and women in the Old Testament have important roles in advancing God's dream, but none more important than Abraham. He is God's choice to build a clan, a nation and a world-wide family of image-bearers.

Abraham begins a bloodline of a special people; Israel. Through this chosen family, God plans to recapture the dream.

Abraham's Call

> *Now the Lord said to Abram, "Go from your country and your kindred and your father's house to the land that I will show you. And I will make of you a great nation, and I will bless you and make your name great, so that you will be a blessing. I will bless those who bless you, and him who dishonors you I will curse, and in you all the families of the earth shall be blessed."* (Genesis 12:1-3)

Verse 4 begins with *"So Abram went."* I wonder what spiritual preparation Abram possessed to enable him to first hear the one true God and then have the faith to obey. He lived in a pagan land filled with people worshipping idols and false Gods.

Abraham's Covenant
What does God promise Abraham?

1. Land for Abraham's family

God promised Abraham land. A place where his family would grow and prosper, while they worshipped the one true God.

As we follow the story we learn that God uses the land as a blessing for obedience and a judgment for disobedience. Examples of blessing can be found at its highest point during the reign of David and Solomon. Examples of judgment are the Assyrian and Babylonian invasions.

Was there a time in history when the promise of the land was fulfilled?

> *And now I am about to go the way of all the earth, and you know in your hearts and souls, all of you, that not one word has failed of all the good things that the Lord your God promised concerning you. All have come to pass for you; not one of them has failed. But just as all the good things that the Lord your God promised concerning you have been fulfilled for you, so the Lord will bring upon you all the evil things, until he has destroyed you from off this good land that the Lord your God has given you, if you transgress the covenant of the Lord your God, which he commanded you, and go and serve other gods and bow down to them. Then the anger of the Lord will be kindled against you, and you shall perish quickly from off the good land that he has given to you."* (Joshua 23:14-15)

According to this passage, how many of God's promises failed to come to pass? None, all were fulfilled. If the old covenant people failed to keep the covenant, what was to be their punishment? They were removed from the land. The first exodus from the land happened when the 10 Tribes of Israel were captured and taken out of the land and never returned.

The Second exodus was for the remaining two tribes; this happened when Babylon came and removed them from the land. From this exile, only a small remnant returned to rebuild Jerusalem and the Temple.

Apostle Paul wrote how the land promises were fulfilled under the New Covenant.

> *For the promise to Abraham and his offspring that he would be heir of the world did not come through the law but through the righteousness of faith.* (Romans 4:13)

Apostle Paul takes the original promise of land and expands it to the entire world. Now not only Israel has a promise, but all nations. This is one reason why the church must be about 'making disciples of all nations,' so they can enjoy the blessings of Abraham.

Many Christians believe it is mandatory to support modern Israel in their possession of land, because of the covenant with Abraham. How do the Apostles of the New Testament deal with this issue? Are there any passages in the New Testament where the old covenant land promise is renewed? There are none that I can find. If Christians want to support modern day Israel in their possession of the land, do so for political reasons not from a Scriptural mandate.

2. To be a 'Great Nation'
During the reign of David and his son Solomon, Israel possessed the land and became a great nation. The temple was one of the great wonders of the world.

3. Be blessed of God and have a 'Great Name'
There is no doubt Abraham was blessed by God and his name was one of the greatest names in human history. Today we have three faiths - Judaism, Christianity and Islam - all holding Abraham in high esteem.

4. All the families of the earth will be blessed
God promised Abraham that his seed would bless the world. The original promise was beyond creating a single nation; the whole world was to be blessed through Abraham.

The Seed of Abraham
One of the great questions which intersects every doctrine is "Who are the sons of Abraham?" The story and promise to Abraham has rich eschatological overtones. If the promises contained in the covenant with Abraham were only for one nation, then our understanding of the Gospel and how it moves through history must be examined in this light. On the other hand, if the Gospel preached by Jesus was for all humanity and God's goal was to transform all nations, then we have a very different eschatology; a victorious one. The implications of the Abrahamic Covenant are huge in determining our purpose and mission.

Dispensational scholars claim the promises to Abraham can only be fulfilled by ethnic Israel, the old covenant people of God. To accommodate this in the present time, they create two peoples of God, who occupy different ages. Today, the church is working to preach the Gospel and save souls for heaven, and then later (during the 1,000-year millennial kingdom) Israel will fulfill all the promises given to Abraham.

L.S. Chafer, a prominent dispensational theologian writes: "The dispensationalist believes that throughout the ages God is pursuing two distinct purposes: one related to the earth with earthly people and earthly objectives involved, which is Judaism; while the other is related to heaven with a heavenly people and heavenly objectives involved, which is Christianity." [2]

Is this two peoples / two ages doctrine taught anywhere by Jesus or the New Testament Apostles? I can find no evidence. In fact, the opposite is seen throughout the new covenant Scriptures. Israel, Jews, Gentiles (free or slaves, men and women) - everyone is included in the Gospel (the good news of the arriving kingdom).

"Even so Abraham believed God, And it was reckoned to him as righteousness. Therefore, be sure that it is those who are of faith who are the sons of Abraham. The Scripture, foreseeing that God would justify the Gentiles by faith, preached the gospel beforehand to Abraham, saying, All nations will be blessed in you. So then those who are of faith are blessed in you." (Galatians 3:6-9)

"For the promise to Abraham or to his descendants that he would be heir of the world was not through the law, but through the righteousness of faith. For if those who are of the law are heirs, faith is made void and the promise is nullified... For this reason it is by faith, in order that it may be in accordance with grace, so that the promise will be guaranteed to all the descendants, not only to those who are of the Law, but also to those who are of the faith of Abraham, who is the father of us all." (Romans 4:13-14 & 16)

These two passages make it very clear; God's promise to Abraham will NOT be fulfilled through the Law (the old covenant) but by a people of faith (people of the new covenant). Paul makes it clear; those who receive the promises are those who have experienced grace through faith. Those who are "of faith" are the redeemed in Christ. These new believers in the Messiah are now positioned to be the beneficiaries of the promises made in the Old Testament.

"In order that in Christ Jesus the blessing of Abraham might come to the gentiles, so that we would receive the promise of the Spirit through faith." (Galatians 3:1)

"Now the promises were spoken to Abraham and to his seed. He does not say, And to seeds, as referring to many, but rather to one, And to your seed, that is, Christ." (Galatians 3:16)

Who are the children of Abraham?

"For he is not a Jew who is one outwardly, nor is circumcision that which is outward in the flesh, But he is a Jew who is one inwardly; and circumcision is that which is of the heart, by the Spirit, and not by the letter; and his praise is not from men, but from God." (Romans 2:28-29)

The ministry of Jesus in His death and resurrection creates a new Israel. Jesus began His ministry by choosing 12 men, which was a sign to the nation, of His intentions. At the beginning of His ministry Jesus was constituting a new Israel. The Jews were not excluded, they were the first chosen.

"For neither is circumcision anything, nor uncircumcision, but a new creation. And those who will walk by this rule, peace and mercy be upon them, and upon the Israel of God." (Galatians 6:15-16)

My conclusion is that I have not found a single New Testament Scripture where God intends to re-establish the old covenant with ethnic Israel. Nor is there any promise that affirms the physical land of Palestine belongs to them as an ongoing covenant promise. God does indeed have a people, the church of Jesus Christ, made up of Jews and Gentiles alike. Since the blessing of Abraham is given to the people of the new circumcision, then the church has a commission to bring these blessings to the nations of the world. Concerning the promise of the land, that also is renewed from a small piece of the earth to the entire earth (Rom. 4:13).

Abraham's Dream

By faith Abraham obeyed when he was called to go out to a place that he was to receive as an inheritance. And he went out, not knowing where he was going. By faith he went to live in the land of promise, as in a foreign land, living in tents with Isaac and Jacob, heirs with him of the same promise. For he was looking forward to the city that has foundations, whose designer and builder is God. (Hebrews 11:8-10)

What city under the new covenant has foundations?

So then you are no longer strangers and aliens, but you are fellow citizens with the saints and members of the household of God, built on the foundation of the apostles and prophets, Christ Jesus himself being the cornerstone, in whom the whole structure, being joined together, grows into a holy temple in the Lord. In him you also are being built together into a dwelling place for God by the Spirit. (Ephesians 4:19-22)

Abraham was looking for the true people of God; the church!

Discussion and Questions

1. Discuss the statement "God is transforming the world through Israel." Is this still true?
2. According to 'Dispensationalism' how will God fulfill the Abrahamic Covenant?
Some Christians teach there will never be peace in Israel until Jesus returns. Is this true? How does it affect our understanding of the churches' mission in the world?

3. Can we be supporters of Israel and the same time support the Palestinians?

4. Are there aspects of the promises made with Abraham that remain to be fulfilled?

Footnotes
[2] L.S. Chafer, Dispensationalism, Dallas Seminary Press, 1936, page 107.

Lesson 4
A People Become a Nation - Moses and the Law

Moses is the unwilling hero. He would have rather tended sheep and goats in the mountains than face off with the supreme ruler of Egypt. Nevertheless, the hand of God puts him at the right place at the right time. Under Jacob, the promised family of Abraham ends up in Egypt and grows into a sizeable nation, a nation in slavery.

How can this 'chosen nation' serve God while in slavery? It cannot, therefore God ordains a deliverer; Moses. We know the story of how God delivered His people out of Egypt and by miracle after miracle they become a free people. They became free from Egypt, but they were not free from their own fears and misgivings concerning this God, who brought them and left them in a dessert.

Now, Moses moves from the mighty deliverer to a true statesman, who brings the children of Jacob into being the covenant people of God. How will this people be distinguished from other nations? They will have God's Laws. Moses and his Law are a dividing point as to how we view the covenants. Are Christians obligated to keep all or parts of the Mosaic Law? How does this covenant, established with the nation of Israel work once Jesus comes to earth? The relationship between law and grace, Moses and Jesus, has been debated for ages, yet it is necessary for our understanding of the Bible to sort this out as best as we can.

> *"Do not think that I have come to abolish the Law or the Prophets; I have not come to abolish them but to fulfill them. For truly, I say to you, until heaven and earth pass away, not an iota, not a dot, will pass from the Law until all is accomplished."* (Matthew 5:17-18)

31

In these verses we have one of the most difficult passages in the Bible. If we survive a rigorous examination of these words and come away with a few useful hermeneutical tools (principles of interpretation), it will serve us well as we continue to study the New Testament.

Jesus makes a statement that seems simple enough; the Law is in effect until heaven and earth pass away. Look out the window, see the sky and earth. Since everything is still here, the logical conclusion should be, we remain under the complete law of Moses.

But that creates even greater problems. We must examine some alternative ways to understand what Jesus meant.

It is here where eschatology and covenant abruptly collide (or better said, they intentionally blend together). There is a time element we must determine (eschatology) and we have the conditionals for righteousness (covenant). We begin with the word 'fulfill.'

What does it mean to *fulfill* the Law and the Prophets? We know one thing for sure - it does not mean *abolish*. *Fulfill* is the opposite to *abolish*. There are several options available.

1. Jesus was referring to the literal heavens and earth, therefore, the Law of Moses in its entirety is binding. We remain under the Law.

2. The Mosaic Law must be seen in three parts; the ceremonial law, the civil law and the moral law. The moral law of Moses remains, whereas the first two passed away with the coming of Christ.

3. The terms "heaven and earth" are covenantal terms which represent the old and new covenant. Therefore, when the old covenant finally passes away, it is the same as saying the old creation - heaven and earth - passes away. With the arrival of the new covenant (a new heaven and earth) the Mosaic Law has found its fulfillment and has no binding authority, since it represents the old heaven and earth.

4. The Mosaic Law is not binding on Christians but will return in the 1,000-year millennium, where the Jews will keep the old law. This is the approach most dispensationists take. It is postponed for a future time.

A Case for the Mosaic Law passing away with the coming of the New Covenant

1. If the Mosaic Law was 'abolished' it would have been like it never existed. Therefore, it would have no future value of any kind. Even though the Law is not binding, it is still useful. Why? Because both the Law and the Prophets speak of Jesus (Luke 24:44). Our study of Moses and the Prophets will continue to be profitable as we seek to see Jesus, in type, poetry, shadow, prophecy, and symbols. Just look. Jesus and the results of the new covenant can be found all though the Old Testament.

2. If the Law of Moses was to be a continual authoritative law, then, how could ALL the Law be kept once the temple was torn down?

3. The literal heaven and earth remain intact, but there was a change of covenants in the ministry of Jesus. The change was so radical that Apostle Paul calls it *a new creation*.

4. We must pay attention that it is not only Moses and the Law which Jesus is speaking about; it is also the Prophets. If the Prophets were to be abolished, then the coming of Jesus, the new covenant and salvation, is a complete new thing, which is separate from the story of Israel. This is not how the first century Apostles viewed the coming of Jesus. Jesus came as the son of David and the son of Abraham. He came within the story of Israel in order to bring fulfillment to it. The Law and the Prophets cannot be abolished, but they must be fulfilled.

5. If we see the word 'fulfill' not as an act of abolishment but as 'for the purpose of' I believe we get to the heart of the context and meaning. Jesus came and completed the story of natural Israel.

33

He came for this purpose, to be the 'faithfulness of God.' He came and revealed that God had not forgotten Israel and the covenant promises. He was the answer and now would fulfill all things. If we erased the Old Testament, (Law & Prophets) Jesus would have no context for His coming. The fulfillment is in the person of Jesus to which the law pointed. He is the fulfillment of everything Moses and the Prophets spoke of. How could He abolish the written word of God? He did not come to abolish but to fulfill. It is necessary to see the Law and the Prophets as the body of Scripture pointing to Israel's Messiah.

Abolish

Jesus said he did not come to abolish the law. Yet Apostle Paul wrote in Romans 7:4 that we have "died to the Law" and in 7:6 we are 'released from the Law.' The word translated 'released' is the same word in Ephesians 2:15 (katargéō) where it is translated as 'abolished.'

Thayer's Definition of 'Katargeo': "*to render idle, unemployed, inactivate, inoperative, to cause a person or thing to have no further efficiency, to deprive of force, influence, power, to cause to cease, put an end to, do away with, annul, abolish.*"

Apostle Paul uses some strong words to describe the Mosaic Law and its use for new covenant believers. Considering what Jesus said, Paul must have had some revelation from the Holy Spirt in order to make sense of this.

Final argument: Those who claim the Mosaic Law, at least in part, is still binding upon Christians, forget one important thing. The new covenant life cannot be lived in the flesh. Living in the glorious new covenant can only be done in the Holy Spirit. It is a completely supernatural lifestyle. Even an unbeliever can keep the Law of Moses but not the Law of Christ. Keeping laws can be done by simple obedience, a matter of willpower. Apostle Paul makes this clear in II Corinthians 3:3-6.

And you show that you are a letter from Christ delivered by us, written not with ink but with the Spirit of the living God, not on tablets of stone but on tablets of human hearts. Such is the confidence that we have through Christ toward God. Not that we are sufficient in ourselves to claim anything as coming from us, but our sufficiency is from God, who has made us sufficient to be ministers of a new covenant, not of the letter but of the Spirit. For the letter kills, but the Spirit gives life.

Discussion and Questions

1. If Jesus meant the literal heaven and earth in Matthew 5:18 then how would that work under the new covenant?

2. Discuss the various definitions of the word 'fulfill.'

3. If Christians think it is imperative to keep portions of the Mosaic Law what difference does it make?

4. Why is it vital to the Christian faith that the Holy Spirit has a central role in working holiness in our lives? What is holiness? Is it a process or instant at our salvation?

Lesson 5
King David - A Preview
of the Coming Attraction

David, like Abraham, has a central role in the family of Israel to bring forth the Messiah. While many of the Old Testament leaders filled vital positions, the New Testament Apostles use both Abraham and David to explain the 'good news' of the kingdom of God (Mt. 1:1). They bring continuity to the story of Israel. God did not forget Israel.

> *"Your house and your kingdom shall endure before me forever; your throne shall be established forever"* (II Samuel 7:16)

In the book of Psalms, the promise is repeated.

> *"I have made a covenant with My chosen; I have sworn to David My servant, I will establish your seed forever And build up your throne to all generations."* (Psalms 89:3)

This is a great promise. The family and reign of David's descendants will never cease. The problem was that after Solomon died, the kingdom was divided and eventually ended.

How can this prophecy be true, when the sons of David failed to maintain his reign? The only way this can be understood is by reading how the apostles of the New Testament interpreted it.

> *"Brothers, I may say to you with confidence about the patriarch David that he both died and was buried, and his tomb is with us to this day. Being therefore a prophet, and knowing that God had sword with an oath to him that he would set one of his descendants on his throne,*

he foresaw and spoke about the resurrection of the Christ, that he was not abandoned to Hades, nor did his flesh see corruption. This Jesus God raised up, and of that we all are witnesses. Being therefore exalted at the right hand of God, and having received from the Father the promise of the Holy Spirit, he has poured out this that you yourselves are seeing and hearing. For David did not ascend into the heavens, but he himself says, "'The Lord said to my Lord, Sit at my right hand, until I make your enemies your footstool.' Let all the house of Israel therefore know for certain that God has made him both Lord and Christ, this Jesus whom you crucified." (Acts 2:29-36)

How did Peter understand the words of David? We know David was known to be a great king, but Peter called him a *prophet*. He looked ahead and saw Christ and His resurrection. It is Jesus (the Messiah) that is the legitimate heir to David's throne.

Jesus is now reigning from the throne of David in the heavens over all creation!

Scripture points to a spiritual fulfillment, not a natural one. Jesus is not physically seated in Jerusalem, yet for Peter the resurrection proves He was seated at the right hand of God and His kingdom reign had begun.

The throne of David represents the authority Jesus received at the ascension. Peter understood the promises to King David were now being fulfilled in the resurrection of Jesus.

This is a fatal blow to any postponement theory and the creation of a millennial kingdom in the future. If Jesus is now (from the time of the resurrection and ascension) reigning as king from the throne of David, then the kingdom of God is in session.

The dispensational scheme claims Jesus offered the kingdom to Israel but later (upon Israel's rejection) postponed that offer. The kingdom now waits in heaven, until the second coming of Jesus. Therefore, we are not in the age of the kingdom, it is in the future. This is called the postponement theory and it is vital to the maintaining of their premillennial eschatology. If Jesus is now seated on David's throne (as Peter believed) then the kingdom has begun and best of all - the Kingdom is here!

> *"That he worked in Christ when he raised him from the dead and seated him at his right hand in the heavenly places, far above all rule and authority and power and dominion, and above every name that is named, not only in this age but also in the one to come."* (Ephesians 1:20-21)

Paul is convinced that Jesus is seated at the right hand of God. This is the same thing as sitting on a throne. Whoever sits on the throne has *"all rule and authority and power and dominion."*

> *"He is the radiance of the glory of God and the exact imprint of his nature, and he upholds the universe by the word of his power. After making purification for sins he sat down at the right hand of the Majesty on high."* (Hebrews 1:3)

> *"The Lord says to my Lord, Sit at my right hand until I make your enemies a footstool for your feet."* (Psalm 110:1)

Psalms 110 is the most quoted Old Testament passage in the New Testament!

It is important, because it speaks directly about Christ's fulfilling the role of King, based on the Davidic covenant.

The ascension of Christ assures us that all authority has been given to Him. Christ is presently seated at the right hand of the Father, and He is ruling over His kingdom through His church. The enemies of Christ are now being subdued. One by one, they are falling before the king.

Will the throne of David endure forever? Yes, it will! Yet, this can only be true if king David is but a representative of the true King David, Jesus Christ.

"And I will make him the firstborn,
the highest of the kings of the earth.
My steadfast love I will keep for him forever,
and my covenant will stand firm for him.

I will establish his offspring forever
and his throne as the days of the heavens.

Once for all I have sworn by my holiness;
I will not lie to David.
His offspring shall endure forever,
his throne as long as the sun before me."

The throne of David, which Jesus now occupies, is forever. The increase of Christ's reign is a promise to all generations. The kingdom of God is advancing. Believe for increase! We should pray that the "throne of David" (which is the seat of Godly government) would increase in our communities. We can expect greater things, because Jesus reigns. The generations to come should expect greater things. The pessimistic worldview that sees evil increasing is not a biblical one. Jesus is on the throne of God, and His reign through the church marches victoriously through history.

"Simeon has related how God first concerned
Himself about taking from among the Gentiles
a people for His name. With this the words of
the Prophets agree, just as it is written, 'After

40

*these things I will return, and I will rebuild
the Tabernacle of David which has fallen."*
(Acts 15:14-16)

This section in Acts is pivotal because it shows how we
should interpret promises made in the Old Testament. James
is summarizing the argument about the status of the Gentiles
in the new Christian church. He quotes a passage out of
Amos speaking about rebuilding the Tabernacle of David.
Let us see exactly what Amos prophesies and then how
James applies the prophecy in light of the New Covenant.

> *"In that day I will raise up the fallen booth of
> David, And wall up is breaches; I will also
> raise up its ruins and rebuild it as in the days
> of old...Behold, the days are coming, declares
> the Lord, 'When the plowman will overtake
> the reaper and the treader of grapes him who
> sows seed; And the mountains will drip sweet
> wine and all the hills will be dissolved...And I
> will plant them on their land and they will not
> again be rooted out from their land which I
> have given them,' says the Lord your God."*
> (Amos 9: 11, 13, 15)

Amos prophesies that the tabernacle of David will be
restored. This restoration includes Israel being planted back
into their land with a great blessing upon it. The passage
seems clear, Israel as a nation is to be restored to the physical
land. There is only one problem; James interprets this
passage entirely different. James does not tell us to expect
Israel to regain sovereignty and rebuild her temple. He uses
Amos as a proof text for God's intention to save Gentiles.
The rebuilding of David's tabernacle is not a temple of stone,
but of people, Jews and Gentiles alike. The revival
prophesied in natural terms is to be fulfilled in a harvest of
souls among the Gentiles. The hills (representing human
kingdoms) will give way to the one mountain of God, Mount

Zion. This passage is one of the clearest in teaching how the church fulfills Old Testament prophecy.

Discussion and Questions

1. Does restoring the 'Tabernacle of David' involve more than Gentiles being added to God's people? Discuss the worship arrangements in David's tent. Who was included? Who was excluded? Was the presence of God available to all who entered?

2. How would we explain the spiritual throne of David to people who insist it is a physical throne that must be built in our future?

3. Why do you think the phrase 'At the right hand of God' is used so much in the New Testament?

4. How can the church build up the throne of David?

Lesson 6
Isaiah and the King

The Prophet Isaiah was a kingdom prophet. Throughout his book we have multitudes of images, word pictures, poems, and prophetic declarations concerning the coming Messiah.

> *For to us a child is born, to us a son is given; and the government shall be upon his shoulders, and his name shall be called Wonderful Counselor, Might God, Everlasting Father, Prince of Peace.* (Isaiah 9:6)

We can only speculate as to how the people of God in Isaiah's day understood this prophecy. There was a growing conviction that Israel's troubles could only be solved if God (in personal power and presence) would intervene. In this passage Isaiah reveals that when this 'child is born' he would have God-like qualities. This must have confused the people of Israel, especially when the names "Mighty God" and "Everlasting Father" were ascribed to Him.

Yet, it was a source of deep comfort and faith, that their God, Israel's God would come to their recuse. For Israel it was more than God sending a servant, or a messenger, or even the Messiah, but that God Himself would come. As Christians we understand this came about in the incarnation of Jesus. He was God coming and the Son that was given. Jesus was the God-man.

> *He came to his own, and his own people did not receive him.* (John 1:11)

To understand the New Testament, we must recognize that what we read is the continuation of Israel's story. Far too often we close the book of Malachi thinking the end has come or has been 'postponed' far in the future.

This is foundational to dispensational theology. In this line of teaching God will once again continue his work with Israel, once the church is removed from the earth (by a secret rapture). The authors of the New Testament had another version and so did Jesus. Jesus did not arrive on earth to begin something different from what He was doing in the nation of Israel, but to fulfill everything promised throughout the hundreds of years of her history. The prophets had spoken. Now, the time is here; the day of fulfillment.

As a nation, John tells us they *"received Him not."* This is the sad part of the story. The greatest generation in human history, the time God walked among us in human flesh, and most of His own people did not recognize it. Yet, some did, and this 'remnant', as Apostle Paul calls them, received what was promised. Israel would be restored and be the light to the nations. But not the Israel with geographic borders, or the Israel which only accepted the Mosaic Covenant. The fulfillment was given to Israel, but the new and reformed Israel now centered around the Messiah. The new covenant would govern this reign of God's kingdom.

> *Of the increase of his government and of peace there will be no end, on the throne of David and over his kingdom. To establish it and to uphold it with justice and with righteousness from this time forth and for evermore. The zeal of the Lord of hosts will do this.* (Isaiah 9:7)

The head of this government is no less than a David-like king. He would sit on the throne of David to rule over his kingdom. Justice and righteousness were the hallmarks of the kingdom.

> *Your throne, O God, is forever and ever. The scepter of your kingdom is a scepter of uprightness; you have loved righteousness and hated wickedness.*

Therefore God, your God, has anointed you with the oil of gladness beyond your companions. (Psalms 45:6-7, see Hebrews 1:8-9)

For as the earth brings forth its sprouts, and as a garden causes what is sown in it to sprout up, so the Lord GOD will cause righteousness and praise to sprout up before all the nations. (Isaiah 61:11)

The Bible is clear. Righteousness and Worship would spring forth in all nations.

Jeremiah is often wrongly seen as the only Old Testament prophet who saw and wrote concerning the future new covenant. Throughout these two chapters, Isaiah writes a beautiful poem filled with amazing insights into a future covenant that God would establish among His people. He begins by declaring the children of *"the desolate one"* will be greater than the children of the *"married"* one. It was the nation Israel who was *'married'* to God. Who are the children of the desolate? They are the gentile peoples, all those from other nations. Isaiah then tells the people of God that their *'tents'* must be enlarged. Why? Because there will be a tremendous growth. The offspring of these gentile believers will *'possess the nations.'* We know this inclusion of gentiles and their amazing growth takes place under the new covenant. Isaiah calls this arrangement a *'covenant of peace'* (Is. 54:10) and an *'everlasting covenant'* (Is. 55:8).

For Zion's sake I will not keep silent, and for Jerusalem's sake I will not be quiet, until her righteousness goes forth as brightness, and her salvation as a burning torch. 2 The nations shall see your righteousness, and all the kings your glory, and you shall be called by a new name that the mouth of the LORD will give. (Isaiah 62:1-2)

45

There shall come forth a shoot from the stump of Jesse, and a branch from his roots shall bear fruit. 2 And the Spirit of the LORD shall rest upon him, the Spirit of wisdom and understanding, the Spirit of counsel and might, the Spirit of knowledge and the fear of the Lord. (Isaiah 11:1-2)

In these verses, we are told that the Holy Spirit would rest upon the Messiah. Jesus walked in the fullness of the Spirit and He opened the door for us to follow. The Christian life is a walk in the Spirit. Attempting to live in the kingdom by any other means is utterly useless. All attempts will fail. To live in the Kingdom of God we must learn to be continually filled, walk in, and be led by the Holy Spirit.

For I will pour water on the thirsty land, and streams on the dry ground; I will pour my Spirit upon your offspring, and my blessing on your descendants. (Isaiah 44:3)

Who will be filled with the Spirit of God and advance the kingdom? Those who are thirsty. Those who will settle for nothing less than God's best.

Isaiah wrote one of the most controversy passages in the Bible.

"For behold, I create new heavens and a new earth, and the former things shall not be remembered or come into mind. But be glad and rejoice forever in that which I create; for behold, I create Jerusalem to be a joy, and her people to be a gladness. I will rejoice in Jerusalem and be glad in my people; no more shall be heard in it the sound of weeping and the cry of distress. No more shall there be in it an infant who lives but a few days, or an old man who does not fill out his days, for the young man shall die a hundred years old, and

the sinner a hundred years old shall be accursed. They shall build houses and inhabit them; they shall plant vineyards and eat their fruit. They shall not build and another inhabit; they shall not plant and another eat; for like the days of a tree shall the days of my people be, and my chosen shall long enjoy the work of their hands. The wolf and the lamb shall graze together; the lion shall eat straw like the ox, and dust shall be the serpent's food. They shall not hurt or destroy in all my holy mountain," says the Lord. (Isaiah 65:17-22 &25)

Is this a portrayal of heaven? Did Isaiah see the future 1,000-year millennium like dispensationalists believe? Or, is this a prophetic declaration about the extent of the kingdom of God in its advancement in the earth? No matter how literal or symbolic we interpret this passage, it shows more than any other Scripture, true kingdom-like conditions. I believe Isaiah shows us that once the 'Son is given" and His reign begins, then, nothing can stop the advance of His kingdom, until these conditions of peace, safety, productivity, joy and gladness, fill the earth.

Discussion and Questions

1. How literal or symbolic should we interpret Isaiah 65? Even if there are symbolic metaphors, what are their meanings? When will these conditions take place? Is this before or after the 'resurrection of the dead?'

2. What are some ways God is using to cause 'righteousness and praise to sprout up before all the nations?'

3. How do you think a 'dispensationists' would interpret Isaiah 9:7?

4. What were the consequences of Jesus' own people rejecting him?

Lesson 7
The New Covenant

Have you dreamed of being a biblical character? Is so, Jeremiah, more than likely would be low on your list. He was called a prophet to the nations and yet, he spent much of his life in one location and was persecuted for the word he spoke. His word from God was the opposite of what the people wanted to hear.

Despite the opposition and the dreary conditions he suffered under, it was Jeremiah who prophesied the new covenant with clarity. Through his blurred teary eyes, he saw hope.

> *"Behold, the days are coming, declares the Lord, when I will make a new covenant with the house of Israel and the house of Judah, not like the covenant that I made with their fathers on the day when I took them by the hand to bring them out of the land of Egypt, my covenant that they broke, though I was their husband, declares the Lord.*

> *For this is the covenant that I will make with the house of Israel after those days, declares the Lord: I will put my law within them, and I will write it on their hearts. And I will be their God, and they shall be my people. And no longer shall each one teach his neighbor and each his brother, saying, 'Know the LORD,' for they shall all know me, from the least of them to the greatest, declares the Lord. For I will forgive their iniquity, and I will remember their sin no more."* (Jeremiah 31:31-34)

> *But as it is, Christ has obtained a ministry that is as much more excellent than the old as the covenant he mediates is better, since it is enacted on better promises. For if that first covenant had been faultless, there would have been no occasion to look for a second. For he finds fault with them when he says: "Behold, the days are coming, declares the Lord, when I will establish a new covenant with the house of Israel and with the house of Judah* (Hebrews 8:6-8)

The subject of the new covenant is vast in scope, yet, we want to cover some basic elements as they apply to Jeremiah's prophecy.

1. The old covenant was with 'faults.'
2. The new covenant is a walk in the Spirit rather than obedience to a written law.
3. The new covenant has no generational curses (read Jer. 31:29-30).
4. The new covenant brings everyone into the knowledge of the Lord.
5. The new covenant and the Law of God.

Jeremiah says under the new covenant God will put His law within the people. The question I have and one that gets avoided in most discussions is, "What Law was God writing on the hearts of new covenant believers"? If we would have asked this question to Jeremiah in his day, the question would have seemed foolish. I think his answer would have been, "The Mosaic Law, there is no other law." Until the coming of Jesus there was only the laws God Moses. That works well, until we get to the New Testament.

Which Law was Apostle Paul under?

For though I am free from all, I have made myself a servant to all, that I might win more of them. To the Jews I became as a Jew, in order to win Jews. To those under the law I became as one under the law (though not being myself under the law) that I might win those under the law. To those outside the law I became as one outside the law (not being outside the law of God but under the law of Christ) that I might win those outside the law.
(I Corinthians 9:19-21)

When Paul was ministering to his fellow Jews he acted like the Jews of his day. He states, "*I became as one under the law.*" Yet, Paul goes out of his way in writing to not allow anyone to think that as believer in Christ, he was still under the Mosaic Law.

When he was with Gentiles with no knowledge or practice of the Mosaic Law he says, he was like those who were '*outside the law.*' Yet, he needed to make sure his readers did not misunderstand and think he was living completely free of God's laws, so he stated he was '*under the law of Christ.*' This is the law of God written on people's hearts when they come to Christ.

Without learning about love, they sense a greater love within. Without knowing about righteousness, they want to live to please God. The moral law of God is written in our hearts. The more we walk by the Spirit, the more we live according to everything God desires of us. Attempting to obey lists of laws, even New Testament laws, ends with failure, unless we are empowered by the Spirit and walk in the true law of Christ.

Brothers, if anyone is caught in any transgression, you who are spiritual should restore him in a spirit of gentleness. Keep watch on yourself, lest you too be tempted. Bear one another's burdens, and so fulfill the law of Christ. (Galatians 6:1-2)

In this passage Apostle Paul links our fulfilling the law of Christ with our service to one another. This outward focus is a key factor under the new covenant. We do not strive constantly after perfection, but look for opportunities to help those in need.

There is therefore now no condemnation for those who are in Christ Jesus For the law of the Spirit of life has set you free in Christ Jesus from the law of sin and death. (Romans 8:1-2)

There is a new covenant law, but it is a law of the Spirit.

Such is the confidence that we have through Christ toward God. Not that we are sufficient in ourselves to claim anything as coming from us, but our sufficiency is from God, who has made us sufficient to be ministers of a new covenant, not of the letter but of the Spirit. For the letter kills, but the Spirit gives life. (II Corinthians 3:4-6)

Apostle Paul often compares walking in the flesh with keeping the law and walking in the Spirit as keeping the law of the new covenant. The first brings death and the last brings life.

Discussion and Questions

1. Why did the people of God need a new covenant?
2. How was the new covenant established?
3. Jeremiah says the new covenant is between God and the '*house of Israel and the house of Judah.*' What about Christians?
4. Read II Corinthians 3:4-11 and discuss the key differences between the old and new covenant.

Such is the confidence that we have through Christ toward God. Not that we are sufficient in ourselves to claim anything as coming from us, but our sufficiency is from God, who has made us sufficient to be ministers of a new covenant, not of the letter but of the Spirit. For the letter kills, but the Spirit gives life. Now if the ministry of death, carved in letters on stone, came with such glory that the Israelites could not gaze at Moses' face because of its glory, which was being brought to an end, will not the ministry of the Spirit have even more glory? For if there was glory in the ministry of condemnation, the ministry of righteousness must far exceed it in glory. Indeed, in this case, what once had glory has come to have no glory at all, because of the glory that surpasses it. For if what was being ended came with glory, much more will what is permanent have glory.

Lesson 8
Daniel and the Dream

If Jeremiah ranks low in our dreams of being a biblical character, then Daniel may be among the highest. Can you dream of being a teenager and being called to stand in front of the king, and impress him? Imagine being in a den of lions and having the supernatural protection of God.

Can you see yourself as a powerful governmental official in a foreign land? Can you imagine having dreams that would predict world changing events hundreds of years in the future? This and much more was the life of Daniel.

For those studying the kingdom for the first time, the book of Daniel is a good place to start (while the book of Revelation is the worst place to start). Three key chapters clearly layout important aspects of how God would bring forth His kingdom on earth and even gives an accurate timeline of when it will happen.

> *You saw, O king, and behold, a great image. This image, mighty and of exceeding brightness, stood before you, and its appearance was frightening. The head of this image was of fine gold, its chest and arms of silver, its middle and thighs of bronze, its legs of iron, its feet partly of iron and partly of clay. As you looked, a stone was cut out by no human hand, and it struck the image on its feet of iron and clay, and broke them in pieces. Then the iron, the clay, the bronze, the silver, and the gold, all together were broken in pieces, and became like the chaff of the summer threshing floors; and the wind carried them away, so that not a trace of them could be found.*

> *But the stone that struck the image became a*
> *great mountain and filled the whole earth.*
> (Chapter 2:31-35)

Daniel interprets the Vision of the king and gives us an eschatological timeline for the arrival of the Messianic Kingdom on earth.

There are four world empires of men, Babylon, Medo-Persia, Greece and Rome. During the final empire, the Roman Empire in the first century, God acts and sends Jesus to establishes His Kingdom.

Dispensational theology, which teaches the kingdom was postponed in the first century, goes to the extreme and needs a revived Roman Empire to make the Messianic Kingdom an event in our future.

Yet, history and Scripture point to the conclusion that Jesus in His incarnation, death and resurrection established the kingdom of God. We are now, two-thousand years into the kingdom and it is growing.

> *And in the days of those kings the God of*
> *heaven will set up a kingdom that shall never*
> *be destroyed, nor shall the kingdom be left to*
> *another people. It shall break in pieces all*
> *these kingdoms and bring them to an end, and*
> *it shall stand forever, just as you saw that a*
> *stone was cut from a mountain by no human*
> *hand, and that it broke in pieces the iron, the*
> *bronze, the clay, the silver, and the gold. A*
> *great God has made known to the king what*
> *shall be after this. The dream is certain, and*
> *its interpretation sure."* (Daniel 2:44-45)

After successive 'kingdoms of men' God says a time will come when He would set up a kingdom. This kingdom, God's kingdom, would be different than all the others. First, all elements of previous kingdoms would be shattered to pieces. We know this occurred at the cross, when Jesus defeated all powers and dominions.

He disarmed the rulers and authorities and put them to open shame, by triumphing over them in him. (Colossians 2:15)

The second difference that distinguishes God's kingdom from all others is that it *'shall stand forever.'*

I saw in the night visions, and behold, with the clouds of heaven there came one like a son of man, and he came to the Ancient of Days and was presented before him. And to him was given dominion and glory and a kingdom, that all peoples, nations, and languages should serve him; his dominion is an everlasting dominion, which shall not pass away, and his kingdom one that shall not be destroyed. (Chapter 7:13-14)

Of the thousands of Bibles passages this is my favorite. Why? Because it describes the Ascension, when Jesus is crowned King. If we get our Christology correct, then understanding our eschatology is much easier. Jesus is King, His kingdom is in session. This began at the Ascension, which led to the royal coronation of a king; the King of kings. Jesus ascends to the Father. His direction is up, not down. This is not a picture of any 'rapture' or the Second Coming.

But the saints of the Most High shall receive the kingdom and possess the kingdom forever, forever and ever. (Daniel 7:18)

There is no doubt in my mind that in verse fourteen the "him" who was given the kingdom is Jesus. He comes up to the Father and receives all authority. Yet, look who else is there; the saints are there! When the Messiah receives the kingdom at the ascension the saints of God also possess the kingdom. To help us understand how the saints function in the kingdom we need to look at Jesus' first action after becoming King. His first action that we know of after the Ascension was to send the Holy Spirit.

Jesus was not alone when He ascended. The New Testament states we are *"seated in heavenly places with Christ"* (Eph. 2:6) Those *"in Christ"* have already received the kingdom. The question is, "What are we doing with the great deposit we have been given?"

> *Seventy week are decreed about your people and your holy city, to finish the transgression, to put an end to sin, and to atone for iniquity, to bring in everlasting righteousness, to seal both vision and prophet, and to anoint a most holy place Know therefore and understand that from the going out of the word to restore and build Jerusalem to the coming of an anointed one, a prince, there shall be seven weeks. Then for sixty-two weeks it shall be built again with squares and moat, but in a troubled time. And after the sixty-two weeks, an anointed one shall be cut off and shall have nothing. And the people of the prince who is to come shall destroy the city and the sanctuary. Its end shall come with a flood, and to the end there shall be war. Desolations are decreed. And he shall make a strong covenant with many for one week and for half of the week he shall put an end to sacrifice and offering. And on the wing of abominations shall come one who makes desolate, until the decreed end is poured out on the desolator.*"

(Chapter 9:24-27)

This passage is called the "Seventy Weeks Prophecy." This one section separates 'Dispensationalism Eschatology' from a 'Victorious Kingdom" position more than any other Scriptural passage. Dispensationalists claim there is a large gap of time between the 69th and 70th week. It is from this passage that they arrive at their "Seven-year Great Tribulation." On closer exanimation it is revealed that there is no evidence for a gap of time during the weeks. Jesus would be crucified in the middle of the 70th week. The amazing aspect of this prophecy is that it provides the people of God with a detailed time table for the arrival of the Messiah and His kingdom. (The starting point is discussed in chapter 9). It would be 490 years, and then the Messiah would come.

Discussion and Questions

1. When does the 'fifth kingdom' begin? What are the primary differences between the fifth kingdom and the previous four?

2. Is there evidence, historically or scripturally, that people in the first century were aware of Daniel's (Ch. 9) prophecy and were looking for and expecting the Messiah?

3. Why in popular evangelical circles is there so much talk of a soon arriving 7-year tribulation period? Is there any Scripture which speaks of this 7-year tribulation? Are there places in the Bible, which give the time-span of the tribulation?

4. How do we explain that after Jesus died and rose from the dead, Rome as a powerful empire continued another three hundred years, when Daniel (Ch.2) wrote that God would bring these empires to an end and break them in pieces?

Lesson 9
Israel Rebuilds the Temple

It was a pagan leader who gave permission for restoring Jerusalem and building the Second Temple. Israel needed permission to rebuild the walls of Jerusalem and then to construct the temple. God was behind the scenes, moving the pieces into alignment, so a faithful remnant would finish their work. The work was slow and there were many enemies. Therefore, God sent prophets to direct and encourage the people.

The Decree to Rebuild
Daniel wrote that from the time of the decree to rebuild Jerusalem until the time of the Messiah, there would be 490 years. We know with a fair amount of accuracy the timing of events in the life of Jesus. His baptism fits very well with the period spoken of in Daniel.

The key question is, when did the prophetic clock began? There were three recorded decrees to rebuild.

The 490 years were to begin *"from the going out of the word to restore and build Jerusalem"* (Daniel 9:25).

1. Cyrus in 538 B.C. (Ezra 1:2-4)
2. Darius in 520 B.C. (Ezra 6:3-12)
3. Artaxerxes in 457 B.C. (Ezra 7:11-26).

My belief when I wrote *Glorious Kingdom* and my current understanding is the same. "Cyrus is a favorite, because there are numerous passages connecting him to a decree for the Jews to return to Jerusalem. Yet, the decree from Artaxerxes better fits the time frame. This decree takes us to the first century during the time of Jesus."

61

Daniel gave the prophecy, but it was Ezra and Nehemiah who led the project of rebuilding Jerusalem and the temple. The temple finally was finished and dedicated to God. Yet, something was missing. There was no powerful presence from heaven like what happened with Solomon's temple. It was like Israel needed a temple, but God was looking forward to the temple of His choice; a temple not of stone, but of human hearts.

What Temple will God abide in?

> And the word of the Lord came to me: "Take from the exiles Heldai, Tobijah, and Jedaiah, who have arrived from Babylon, and go the same day to the house of Josiah, the son of Zephaniah. Take from them silver and gold, and make a crown, and set it on the head of Joshua, the son of Jehozadak, the high priest. And say to him, 'Thus says the Lord of hosts, "Behold, the man whose name is the Branch: for he shall branch out from his place, and he shall build the temple of the Lord. It is he who shall build the temple of the Lord and shall bear royal honor, and shall sit and rule on his throne. And there shall be a priest on his throne, and the counsel of peace shall be between them both. (Zechariah 6:9-13)

This passage has stumped many scholars and commentaries. I have been studying this passage for four years and remain unsure of its meaning and application to the Messiah. Yet, I include it here, because I believe it is an important piece of prophetic literature, which points to Jesus the Messiah and perhaps speaks about the new covenant.

The 'Branch' is the One, who will build the temple. If the Branch refers to the Messiah, then we have here what Jesus said, "*I will build My church*" (Mt.16:18)

The temple God is concerned about is not the 'Second Temple, but the new and living temple. From here the passage gets more complicated.

If we accept that 'the Branch' is the Messiah, as it does in other places (Zech. 3:8, Is. 11:1), then the biggest question is, "Who is the priest?" What is this "Council of peace?" This may be a subtle reference to the new covenant.

That is, if the 'priest' are the people "in Christ," which is the church. Another interpretation is the "Branch" is not the Messiah, but God the Father and the Priest is Jesus (Messiah). If this is the case, it would support the position that the new covenant is between the Father and the Son, instead of being between God and the new Eschatological house of Israel and Judah (with Jesus as the Mediator).

I support that the "Branch" refers to Christ because in the other Old Testament passages it is clear. We also have additional support for this interpretation in the New Testament. In the final chapter of the Bible Jesus speaks of Himself being the Branch (although most English versions translate it offspring or descendant).

> *I, Jesus, have sent my angel to testify to you about these things for the churches. I am the root and the descendant of David, the bright morning star.* (Revelation 22:16)

Hermeneutical Tool: Never allow a passage which is 'not clear' to override similar passages, which are clear.

> *Behold, the man whose name is the Branch: for he shall branch out from his place, and he shall build the temple of the Lord.*

The Branch, the Messiah King, shall build the temple. Within the background of the Second Temple we need to recognize the true will of God, that is the building of the true temple, which is the church.

When Jesus ministered, He often spoke out against the temple, which upset the religious leaders. The temple in Israel's history was the place where heaven and earth met. It was the place of connection between God and His people. When Jesus declared the temple would be left desolate (Mt. 23:38) and later prophesied its destruction (Mt.24:2) we can only image the horror that went through people's thoughts. Especially when their prophet, Zechariah said the 'Branch' would build the temple. The temple Jesus came to build was not a Jewish temple made of stone. Jesus came to build a people. It would be made of 'living stones.'

> *Do you not know that you are God's temple and that God's Spirit dwells in you? If anyone destroys God's temple, God will destroy him. For God's temple is holy, and you are that temple.* (I Corinthians 3:16-17)

This verse is often interpreted as referring to individuals, but Apostle Paul has the church in mind. The 'you' are corporate and plural. Take notice how seriously God protects His temple.

> *As you come to him, a living stone rejected by men but in the sight of God chosen and precious, you yourselves like living stones are being built up as a spiritual house, to be a holy priesthood, to offer spiritual sacrifices acceptable to God through Jesus Christ.* (I Peter 2:4-5)

Apostle Peter joins with Paul in revealing the true nature of the temple. It is a 'spiritual house' built with 'living stones.'

The building of God's true temple, the church, was the focus of the New Testament authors. It is also why in the background throughout the first century there was this waiting and anticipating the destruction of the old temple; just like Jesus prophesied.

Discussion and Questions

1. Why was the Second Temple even built, when God wanted His true temple in the earth?

2. What can we learn about the process of building the Second Temple, when compared to the building up of the church?

3. Has the church today finally understood the nature and function of God's 'spiritual house?'

4. Discuss whether Zechariah 6:9-13 should be used as a supporting text, if the new covenant is between the Father and the Son? Who is the "branch" and who is the "priest?

5. How would you respond, if God said, "My answer to your prayer is you will receive a small portion of it soon, but the bulk of the answer will come in 490 years?"

Lesson 10
400 Years of Prophetic Silence

No one expected there would be a time when no prophets existed. Israel was blessed over the centuries to have a prophetic word from God. Their word was not always heeded, but at least God was speaking, confirming they were the chosen people. Around 400 B.C. a prophetic silence began. No one noticed for a while, the prophets advanced in age and eventually died. But something was different, there were no young prophets emerging. No one to speak for God. How can a nation exist, a covenant nation, a nation God chose for Himself, without an active prophetic voice?

Israel had the Tora to guide them, they had the Psalms to sing and the Prophets to read. Would this be enough to keep them on track? It might be, but the nagging questions lingered, "Has God abandoned us?" "Will He ever speak to us again?" "Will our God keep the covenants He gave us?"

Israel's history did not stop in the years we call 'the silent years' or officially 'the intertestamental period.' This was the time between the Old Testament prophets and when John the Baptist walked among the Jews and declared, *"The kingdom of God is at hand"* (Matt. 3:2)

In brief, here are some important transitions and historical events which shaped the first century.

1. A Time of Peace
The Persian empire ruled from 532 B.C. to 332 B.C. It was Persia that allowed the Jews to return home and rebuilt Jerusalem and the temple. These events are found in the books of II Chronicles and Ezra. The Jews were back home and despite some local opposition, lived in peace, while practicing their ancient religion centered around the temple. This peace would not last forever. A storm was coming.

2. The Abomination

A man from the west was about to change the world, and upset the peace of Israel. He was Alexander the Great, and he defeated Darius, the ruler of Persia. Everywhere he went he exported the culture of Greece. During this time the Hebrew Bible was translated into Greek, which was the primary version in the first century.

Most New Testament quotes used this version called the Septuagint. When you read your New Testament, you will notice that when the authors quote Old Testament verses, it differs from your version of the same passage in the Old Testament. This is because they are reading the Septuagint and our versions are based on different translations.

The Greek culture with its humanistic and worldly behaviors conflicted with the strict lifestyle of the Jews. But the Jews were free to practice their faith.

The rule of Alexander was short and upon his death and after numerous rulers, there arose a ruler so bad, he was known generations later as the "abomination." He name was Antiochus Epiphanes. He wanted no part of the Jews and their religion. In the year 167 B.C., he overthrew the temple priests and did the unthinkable; he sacrificed a pig in the temple. A revolution broke out, a war for freedom had begun. This was the Maccabean revolt.

When Jesus was predicting the fall of Jerusalem and the destruction of the city (Mt.24, Mk.13, Lk 21) he reminded the people of this event and associated it with another '*abomination of desolation*' which would come in their generation.

3. Fulfillment of Daniel

The writings of Daniel are used and abused by many biblical interpreters these days. Yet, many overlook his amazingly accurate prophecy, which came true during the intertestamental period. In chapters ten and eleven we have Israel's near future (300 years) described.

A detailed interpretation would take a book. Most of the prophecies were fulfilled in the 'years of silence.' The descriptions are so vivid and true - when seen from history - that liberal scholars claim it must have been written after the events.

God knows the future and He gave amazing details to Daniel, of events and political circumstances which took place 300 years in the future. Even though there are no written Scripture or active prophets from these years, God was at work in preparing the world for the arrival of His Messiah.

4. Creation of the Pharisees and Sadducees

We could read the entire Old Testament and never learn about the Pharisees and Sadducees. We then open the pages of the New Testament and they are among the central characters. Where did they come from?

Pharisees

"The sect of the Pharisees is thought to have originated in the 3rd century B.C., in days preceding the Maccabean wars, when under Greek domination and the Greek effort to Hellenize the Jews, there was a strong tendency among the Jews to accept Greek culture with its pagan religious customs.

The rise of the Pharisees was a reaction and protest against this tendency among their fellow kinsmen. Their aim was to preserve their national integrity and strict conformity to Mosaic law.

They later developed into self-righteous and hypocritical formalists. Later they were among those who had condemned Jesus to death." [3]

The original goal of the Pharisees was to keep Israel separate and pure from the worldly influence of the Greeks. We always need to keep watch when religious leaders of any day begin to demand the keeping of rules to make us holy and useful to God. Christian character is born out of a life filled with the Holy Spirit.

Sadducees

The sect of the Sadducees was thought to have originated about the same time as the Pharisees. The Sadducees, contrary to the Pharisees, adopted many Greek customs. They wanted no part in the Maccabean struggle for the Jewish nation's independence. They were a priestly sect, and although they were the authoritative religious officials of their nation, they were not very religious. The Sadducees were not very numerous, yet they were very wealthy and influential. The Sadducees controlled the Sanhedrin, even though they were rationalistic and worldly minded.

We can today see viewpoints similar to that of the Pharisees and Sadducees. The Pharisees demanded total separation from culture, whereas the Sadducees advocated adoption of culture while maintaining their ancient faith. Our struggle today should not be if we accept or reject culture, but how can the church be a positive influence and a source of transformation.

5. A Godly Remnant waiting for Israel's Messiah

The New Testament begins with several stories about those waiting and expecting the Messiah. Even during the 'silent years' God was at work and there were always a few who kept the true faith alive. Even though there were no prophets in Israel, God was at work. He was preparing for the greatest generation in human history; the arrival of Israel's Messiah and King over the nations.

> **Zechariah and Elizabeth** *"To make ready for the Lord a people prepared"* (vs. 17). (Luke 1:5-17)

The role of leaders and especially those with prophetic mantels is to prepare people for a fresh moving of God.

> **Mary** *"Behold I am the servant of the Lord; let it be to me according to your word"* (vs. 38). (Luke 1:26-38)

There is nothing better than our submission to the Lord, even when the future is unclear, difficult or confusing.

The Shepherds *"Let us go over to Bethlehem and see this thing that has happened, which the Lord has made known to us"* (vs. 15). (Luke 2:8-20)

Obedience to God even when it is not convenient often leads to great blessing.

Anna *"Waiting for the redemption of Jerusalem"* (vs. 38). (Luke 2:36-38)

Paul said he preached the *'Hope of Israel'* (Acts 28:20) and here Anna was waiting for Jerusalem to be saved. In the natural both failed. Israel lost its temple and Jerusalem was destroyed. Yet, the true redemption of Zion did take place and the dreams of faithful people for centuries WERE fulfilled with the coming of the Messiah.

Discussion and Questions

1. To what extent can the church use modern culture to carry the message of the Gospel?

2. In the Jewish world of the first century two groups played pivotal roles; they were the Pharisees and Sadducees. Discuss how the church has developed other 'religious positions' over the centuries, which have little or no Scriptural support.

3. As individuals we also experience periods in our life where 'God is silent.' What should our attitude be during those times and what can be done to maintain our faith?

4. Like the faithful ones waiting for the Messiah, do we have people today with prophetic foresight, speaking as to what may happen in the next 5, 10, 20 or 50 years? In the Spirit, can there be such a thing of 'reverse engineering?' If we can see aspects (and not perfectly) of what the church and

kingdom will be like in 50 years, then with God's help we can backtrack to see how we get there. Discuss if this could be a legitimate prophetic ministry or just plain, well, a little odd.

Example: A woman in Bulgaria shared two visions, which she received two years apart. She saw Bulgaria 50 years in the future. Whereas now many villages are almost ghost towns and in great poverty, in 50 years they were alive with activity and enjoyed financial prosperity. Artists, craftsmen, and people with unique talents were creating beautiful things and selling them for good prices. She saw rivers and lakes, which were clean. People from other nations were coming to drink the water and in so doing were healed. We need more visions and foresight from God about our future.

Footnotes
[3]Bible History Online (http://www.bible-history.com)

Books by Stan Newton

Glorious Kingdom
A Handbook of Partial Preterist Eschatology

Glorious Kingdom is a comprehensive book on eschatology; kingdom eschatology. In this book Stan Newton takes on dispensational eschatology, which is the position of many evangelicals and lays a foundation from Scripture for a different view. *Glorious Kingdom* covers all major aspects of eschatology with special emphasis on interpreting the prophetic New Testament passages from the viewpoint of the kingdom of God. The kingdom was established by Jesus in the first century. This book will help those seeking biblical answers to tough questions on eschatology.

Glorious Covenant
Our Journey Toward Better Covenant Theology

God is a God of covenants. Christians have a covenant. With these two basic foundations Stan Newton compares contemporary views of covenant. He examines Dispensationalism, Covenant Theology and New Covenant Theology. *Glorious Covenant* finds the fault lines of each position and then through Scriptural discovery argues for a fourth view - Better Covenant Theology. Sadly, many Christians are only vaguely aware of this glorious covenant. How followers of Jesus understand covenant is extremely important and *Glorious Covenant* removes the confusion and presents a clear view of the New Covenant we have in Christ.

Breakfast at Tel Aviv
A Conversation about Israel
Theological Fiction

Shane recently graduated from a Pentecostal Bible school. His future was secure within his denomination except one very large adjustment; he changed his theology. After finishing seminary, he moves back near his hometown church and former pastor, to begin his ministry. Pastor George is waiting for answers.

Over coffee the question is asked, "Shane, you have not abandoned Israel, have you?"

Breakfast in Tel-Aviv is the story of Pastor Shane and Pastor George as they share their positions on Israel. Emotions are high as they regularly discuss their views. Their discussions lead to a trip to Israel and over breakfast all is resolved; or is it?

Kingdom Communion

Kingdom Communion is written with the conviction that we are missing a great opportunity. If we continually see communion as 'not that important', our worship services will fail to make the kingdom transition I believe God is looking for. A revelation of Christ and His advancing kingdom affects every doctrine, and this includes the Lord's Supper. When the church celebrates communion like a wedding we will experience drinking the fourth cup with King Jesus.

All Books are Available on Amazon in Paperback or Kindle Edition

Kingdom Missions
The Ministry of Stan and Virginia Newton

We are singularly focused on teaching and demonstrating the Gospel of the Kingdom as taught in Stan's book, *Glorious Kingdom.* Through Seminars/Bible Schools/Churches we present the view of Christ's present and advancing Kingdom. Stan is available for speaking engagements in your church.

Virginia works in teaching English using a biblical curriculum and in literacy, where she helps develop workbooks to teach people to read.

We need your help in taking this message to the nations. You can E-mail us at svnewton@hotmail.com or become a friend on Facebook.

To send letters or financial gifts please mail to:

Kingdom Missions
PO Box 948
Seattle, WA. 98111

Also, give using PayPal. E-Mail for PayPal is:stannewton@live.com.

80213434R00044

Made in the USA
San Bernardino, CA
24 June 2018